mean the leash is literally loose
mean your dog has to be right a

There is no right or wrong place for your dog to be while walking. It's all a matter of what you prefer and what seems to work best for you and your dog. Some people don't mind if their dogs walk ahead of them a bit as long as the leash is loose. Others prefer their dogs to remain relatively at their side. It's up to you.

Keep in mind that every dog is an individual, and you have to set realistic goals for *your specific dog*. Some dogs are more challenging than others for a variety of reasons such as their age, level of energy, personality, life experience, breed, health and so on.

Some dogs are fearful of unfamiliar places. Some dogs are aggressive to strangers. Some dogs are lazy and some dogs are athletes. And then there are the dogs who are so enthusiastic and *super excited* about everyone and everything! Don't worry, I'm here to help you with some of those issues, too.

This book is designed for all dog owners because no matter where you're at in training, it's always a work in progress. We can always do a little better. At least that's my philosophy, and I hope it's yours too.

Once you've read this ebook, if you'd like to further discuss some of the training topics or if you have additional questions, I welcome you go join our <u>Mighty Paw Fur-lings Group</u> on Facebook.

The <u>Fur-lings group</u> is a good place to ask your training questions, meet other dog owners and get quick feedback from myself and the other members.

It's a team effort, training our dogs!

Let's get started!

-Lindsay

You are part of the Mighty Paw family now! Take **30% off** your next order at MightyPaw.com! Just visit MightyPaw.com/EbookFamily to get your code now!

Table of Contents

Disclaimer

This ebook is written for your reference and is not meant to be exhaustive. It is not meant to replace the value of working directly with a professional dog trainer one-on-one.

No matter what, it's your responsibility to follow safe practices for your own dog and to use common sense when working with dogs.

Before You Start: Goals

Before you begin training your dog not to pull on the leash, here's what I suggest you do first: Write down exactly what your goals are. Be specific.

Do you want your dog to walk with slack in the leash most of the time? Do you want your dog to remain at your left side most of the time? Do you just want him to stop barking and lunging when he sees other dogs? Do you want him to pay attention to you?

Sometimes we focus too much on what we DON'T want our dogs to do (pulling, lunging), and we're not clear on what we WANT them to do instead.

Training your dog for anything can be a difficult and frustrating process for some dog owners so I've found it helpful to take a step back and set an intention for the training. That way when you get frustrated you can look back and remember your original motivations of WHY you decided to do it.

I always ask myself, what is my intention for doing this?

1) I love my dog. I want him to live a happy life and would never want anything bad to happen to him. This is easier if he listens to me and doesn't do things like try to lunge across the road to get to another dog while there's oncoming traffic.

2) I also want my life to be easier and let's face it, life is easier with a dog that listens to you.

3) In order to have these things, I have to spend time training him and that training is probably going to be frustrating.

GOALS & INTENTIONS:

If you're not entirely sure what would be a good goal, there's an acronym called S.M.A.R.T. goals. The acronym stands for the characteristics that good goals have which are: Specific, Measurable, Achievable, Realistic and Time-bound.

This could be an example goal:

I want to get Bailey to stop pulling on the leash when we go for morning walks (Specific/Achievable) and just to walk with a loose-leash within 4 feet of me (Measurable). I want to accomplish this within the next two months (Realistic/Time-bound). By doing this I'll need to come up with some approaches to practice with him (keep reading!) and schedule out 15 mins every other day to work with him on it (Specific/Measurable).

Now with that goal, I can make a serious plan and stick to it! Now it's your turn:

Action Step:

1. Write down 1 or 2 goals for your pup.

2. Write down your intention and WHY you want to train your pup.

Gear You'll Need

The right leash and collar

First things first, make sure you have a collar and leash that help you manage your dog.

There's no reason to make it extra difficult on yourself. *Why struggle when you don't have to?* Get a collar and leash that will help minimize the pulling without hurting your dog.

Martingale collar

We'll discuss more details on gear at the end of this guide, but I recommend a martingale collar and a dual handle leash for starters.

I'll be repeating this throughout this book because it's THAT important!

A martingale collar is also called a "limited slip" collar, and this type of collar is recommended by a large variety of dog trainers. A martingale collar is a good option for a lot of dogs because it will limit your dog's pulling. It is designed to tighten slightly under tension but not so much where it could choke your dog. (By comparison, a slip or choke collar can keep getting tighter and tighter as the dog pulls.)

Since I'm going to show you how to use highly valued food to "lure" your dog, you won't need to give her many "corrections" with this type of collar. At the same time, it also allows you to tug gently to get your dog's attention when needed. Then, you can praise her for paying attention.

A martingale collar also has the added safety benefit of preventing your dog from slipping out of the collar or backing out of the collar and getting away from you. This is because of how it tightens slightly under tension; the dog can't slip out as easily.

You can view our martingale collar at MightyPaw.com.

6-foot dual handle leash

As for a leash, I recommend a 6-foot <u>dual handle leash</u>. This type of leash has a loop handle at the end of the leash like most leashes, but it also has a loop handle closer to your dog's collar (often called a "traffic lead" or "traffic handle").

With this type of leash, you can hold the end of the leash in one hand. Then, when you need a little extra control, you can also grab the second handle with your other hand closer to your dog's collar. This is especially helpful when you have a big dog or a strong "puller."

Every dog is a little different, but those are my top suggestions that will help the largest variety of dogs. However, you know your dog best and sometimes you just have to try a variety of training collars and leashes.

If you have any questions on collars, hop into the Mighty Paw Furlings Group on Facebook and let us know.

Another option: No-pull harness

Typically, a harness is not ideal when you're trying to decrease a dog's pulling. However, if you want to try a harness, use one that has a front clip option. When you can clip the leash to the front of the dog (at his chest), that will limit his ability to pull.

These types of harnesses are often called "no pull" harnesses. They work to decrease a dog's pulling, but keep in mind they are still training TOOLS. We always have to put in the training time!

Use highly motivating treats!

Here's the thing with treats. You need them to be extremely high-value and motivating for your dog when working on difficult concepts like not pulling. Yet, you should also choose treats that are small and easy for your dog to eat. (You can always tear them into smaller pieces.)

Imagine you're at a bar, how much happier is the bartender if you're tipping with $20's instead of $1's? (I'll tell you, a whole lot happier. Same concept applies here.)

Dry dog biscuits would be a poor choice, for example, because they're probably not all that motivating for your dog and they'll also take too long for him to chew. You want something that's roughly the size of a penny or a piece of dry dog food.

When you're training your dog outside, there are tons of distractions, so you're going to need to get creative and use food like bits of string cheese, deli meat torn into small pieces or even pieces of chicken or hamburger.

When I'm training my dog, I mix a variety of treats together in a treat pouch and add in some dry dog food. This keeps things interesting for him!

If you prefer to use actual dog treats instead of meat or cheese, the brand Zuke's minis works well for a lot of dogs. These treats are small, soft and dogs think they smell great!

A treat pouch for holding your dog's treats.

Yes, I highly recommend a <u>treat pouch</u> for training your dog in general but particularly for teaching him to stop pulling. A <u>treat pouch</u> fits around your waist (yep, sort of like a fanny pack!) so you have quick access to treats.

It's very difficult for most dogs to learn not to pull, so you need to be able to reward your dog when he's right at your side doing what you want. Good boy!

Total, I used about <u>a cup of small treats</u> per walk for my 60-pound dog when he was first learning. Obviously, you might need to cut back on your dog's meals if you do this. And no, you will not have to use this many treats **forever**, just while you're first starting out. (Remember, this is very hard for your dog!)

At the very minimum, carry a TON of treats in your pockets but once you start heading out for training walks, you probably won't be able to fit enough treats in your pockets easily. Plus, who wants to be shoving pieces of cheese or chicken in their pockets anyway?

A treat pouch is convenient and keeps grease off your clothes. A treat pouch allows me to walk my dog and give him *treat-treat-treat* for walking at my side. I can fit my whole hand in the pouch so treats are easily accessible at all times.

With the treat pouch, I'm able to reward my dog for:

- looking at you
- walking at your side
- not pulling
- ignoring distractions like other dogs

You can also use treats to lure him back when he pulls or gets ahead.

Our Mighty Paw treat pouch conveniently has a separate pouch for your keys or money, as well as a spot for poop bags.

Action Step:

Grab the products above to help you on your journey. Can you train your dog without these? In all honesty, yeah probably, but these are tools specifically designed to make the process easier on you.

Think of it this way, you definitely can climb a mountain in some classic Vans shoes with a drawstring backpack, but it's definitely easier with hiking boots and a daypack. Don't make hard things harder on yourself.

Here they are again:

- Martingale collar
- 6-foot two handle leash
- "No pull" harnesses (optional)
- Treat pouch
- High-value treats/food

Now, onto the training steps!

How to Stop My Dog From Pulling: 5 Steps

Step 1: You must have a realistic timeline

I'm just throwing this out there because teaching a dog to walk nicely on a leash without pulling is one of **the most difficult concepts** you will ever teach your dog. Keep that in mind while you are training. Be patient and go easy on your dog. This is hard. Sometimes dog owners set unrealistic expectations for their pups and then everyone ends up frustrated.

Dogs are not designed to walk as slow as us. They naturally move at a much, much faster pace and they are driven to check out different scents and sounds.

If you think of the different dog breeds, most of them are bred to do specific work that involves <u>running out ahead of us</u> tracking, flushing, pulling, guarding, herding, hunting or chasing.

It's also not natural for two dogs to walk side by side of each other! You will rarely see this. Instead, dogs speed up, stop, sprint, zig-zag, turn around, you name it!

So when your dog is pulling on the leash, he's not being "bad." He's just being a dog! We have to teach them the fancy "trick" of walking at a painfully slow pace.

As you train your dog not to pull on the leash, you will see some progress very quickly. However, the reality is most dogs are working on loose-leash walking for many months or years. Even then, just because your dog will walk nicely in your own neighborhood does not mean he will walk nicely if you walk in a park or in a different city or wherever it might be.

Walking on a loose leash takes a lot of practice and consistency over a long period of time, so be patient and don't expect miracles! Be easy on yourself and your dog.

Step 2: Practice indoors *a lot*

Outside is just so distracting! It really helps to practice loose-leash walking **at home** in the house and in your own yard.

I worked with my dog in the living room for five minutes a day and it really started to click for him on the third day.

Practicing indoors made a huge difference because my dog seemed to finally "get" what I wanted. With no distractions, it was easy for us to succeed - we both felt proud of ourselves. Always help your dog be successful! Go for the easy wins!

I recommend you work on loose-leash walking with your dog indoors for 15 minutes a day split into 3 short sessions. Because, short attention spans! And we're busy people. I know you're not going to actually do this every single day, but try to make this a goal.

Put a leash on your dog, and wear your <u>treat pouch</u>. Walk along a wall so your dog is between you and the wall. This gives him few options of where to go so he can be successful!

Lure your dog where you want him by holding a treat to his nose and moving forward. I prefer to have my dog on my left side. I hold the end of his leash in my right hand, so the leash is crossed in front of my body. Since my left hand is closer to my dog's nose, that is the hand I use to pop treats into his mouth.

Give your dog treats as long as he is walking on a loose leash generally at your side. Good boy! You don't need to use a verbal cue at this point but if you want to you can start using a word like "heel" or "with me."

Don't worry if your gets ahead of you. They all do this. Just stop moving and lure him back to your side with the treats. You can be very generous with the treats for now. You'll slowly decrease the treat frequency with time. Try to keep this fun, and make sure to stop if you're getting frustrated.

Practice in every room of the house, the basement, the garage, perhaps the back yard or the driveway. Keep it simple!

Tip: Stop often and ask your dog to sit. Then reward with a treat. This will help your dog pay attention and encourage him to stay closer to you. Pop treats in his mouth for being at your side or for making eye contact. Repeat this several times: Take a step, stop, ask your dog to sit, give a treat.

Action Step:

Write down your practice and progress every day.

For example: "Today we practiced loose-leash walking for five minutes in the living room."

Step 3: Practice loose-leash walking outdoors

OK, once your dog is showing some success indoors, you can practice the same concept of loose-leash walking outside in quiet, "boring" areas. Places like your garage, driveway, your own yard and eventually down the street.

Yep, this means you might be walking in circles or turning around a lot or doing figure-8 patterns. Boring is GOOD, because that makes YOU the most interesting thing to your dog at the moment.

Do not forget to use highly motivating treats! Give your dog frequent treats for walking at your side, and make sure to talk to him while you're doing this! *"Wow, what a good boy! Yay! Good boy!"* Now is a good time to start using your "heel" or "with me" or "walk nice" or whatever cue you want to use.

Within a few days or so, you can also think about practicing in other "boring" areas like a nearby parking lot without many cars or foot traffic. I like to practice dog training in church parking lots on weekday mornings because there's rarely anyone there!

Continue to keep your training sessions short to 5 minutes, 10 minutes at the absolute most. Ideally you work for 2 minutes or so, then take a break and let your dog siff for a minute. Then work for another 2 minutes. Remember, this kind of focus is **hard work** for most dogs, especially puppies and younger dogs.

Step 4: Add loose-leash training to your dog's walks

Your dog is probably starting to do pretty well on these short training sessions indoors and in your own backyard, but what about when you actually want to head out for a decent walk? You know, like for real exercise! Something most of our strong "pullers" need!

Teaching a dog not to pull on walks is extremely challenging because:

- Outside, there are just so many distractions! It's very, very difficult for your dog to pay attention to you!

- For some dogs, walking is their main form of exercise. If you live in an apartment like I do, you pretty much have to walk your dog even if he pulls. Therefore, you are "rewarding" him for pulling because you keep moving forward, which is what he wants.

- When you walk in a straight line (like most of us do on walks) our dogs tend to pull harder because they know the route or can anticipate the route.

So here is what I recommend you do on walks:

If you can, provide your dog with some high-intensity exercise in other ways **before** you go for a walk. Things like:

- fetch in the yard
- tug of war
- just running around the yard to burn off energy (play with your dog!)
- allowing your dog to run in an open area on a long leash
- a visit to an off-leash dog park

If your dog has had a chance to run around for a bit *before* you head out for a walk, that will help. Even if you live in an apartment, throwing the ball down the hall a few times or playing tug with a rope toy for 5 minutes can help.

You should also continue practicing your loose-leash walking indoors for 5-minute sessions a few times per day. And, continue to practice this in the immediate areas around your home like your backyard or your apartment hallway.

For walks, unfortunately your dog is still likely to pull at first, especially if he's already been allowed to pull in the past. That's OK.

Here's what you should do for now: Rotate between "training" and "freedom." Let me explain…

Step 5. Take a short break every 2 minutes during walks

On your walks, ask your dog to "heel" or "walk nice" or whatever cue/command you use.

Carry your treat pouch and work with your dog on loose-leash walking for 2 minutes at a time during your walk. During these short sessions, don't allow your dog to pull. Use your treats to lure him like you were doing indoors. Praise him for staying close and maintaining slack in the leash.

If he pulls, simply stop moving forward and lure him back with treats. Or, turn around and walk the other way so he follows.

After just 2 minutes of training, let your dog have some freedom. I don't mean let him off leash. I mean, give him a release word like "break" or "free" and allow him to walk ahead of you and sniff for a few minutes. Hopefully he won't pull *hard* during these breaks but if he does, simply pause or turn around. Keep praising your dog when the leash is loose.

There are a few reasons I like rotating between "training" and "freedom":

- Dogs have short attention spans. I repeat, dogs have short attention spans! Especially certain breeds and puppies.

- Loose-leash walking is *very, very difficult* for dogs. It takes a lot of focus.

- This helps remind you to take breaks and keep this <u>fun!</u>

On your walks rotate every 2 minutes or so between "with me" and "Free!" (Or whatever word/command you want to use.) As your dog is successful, you can make the training sessions 3 minutes, 5 minutes and eventually 10 minutes. But I still recommend you include breaks for your dog. After all, sniffing is fun for them and is even a way to help mentally tire them out.

So, those are my five steps for mastering loose-leash walking and getting control of your dog's pulling. It's definitely a work in progress and you're not going to stop a strong puller overnight or even in a few weeks. This is a work in progress!

Because we could all use some additional suggestions, here are several tips to keep in mind when teaching your dog not to pull on the leash.

Use these to help brainstorm and work through any problems you're having.

Additional tips for loose-leash walking

Tip #1: Don't walk in a straight line all the time.

Walking in a straight line makes it more likely for your dog to pull, so it's actually a good idea to mix things up during training. Be unpredictable so your dog has to pay attention to you!

Walk in figure-8s, zig-zags, randomly turn around or pivot in a circle. Yes, your neighbors might think you look a little crazy. Who cares!

Tip #2: For extremely hard pullers, you might allow some tension.

If your dog is an extra strong puller, you might choose to allow a slight amount of tension in the leash because that's better than the "full force" pulling your dog normally does.

I recommend you determine ahead of time how much pulling you will allow. Once there is more tension in the leash than that, that's when you should stop moving or turn around. When the tension eases, praise your dog and move forward again. As your dog improves, you can allow less and less pulling/tension.

Tip #3: Try two different collars.

Some people choose to clip the leash to a training collar such as a martingale during training sessions and to a harness or standard collar when they are not training.

This works really well for some dogs as it gives them a very clear signal for "working mode" vs. "non working." It's similar to how certain guide dogs or certain police dogs wear a harness when they are working. They know this means business.

However, there are some risks to constantly clipping and unclipping the leash to different collars or harnesses so please be careful so your dog doesn't accidentally get away from you. Make sure your dog is wearing ID tags, and a microchip is also a good idea.

Tip #4: Stop moving when your dog pulls.

If your dog pulls like a train during your walks, you can either stop moving until he lets slack in the leash. However, some dogs will stand there forever with a tight leash and you could literally be there for a half-hour! So, another option is to simply turn around and walk the other way. Turning around will naturally put slack in the leash when your dog turns to follow. Then you can go back to the original direction if you'd like.

Tip #5: Work on random obedience cues during walks.

When you work on random obedience commands like sit, down, stay, come, stand, your dog will be more likely to pay attention to you. Remember to use treats! General obedience training also helps improve your dog's self-control.

Tip #6: Sign up for a basic obedience class.

Practicing in a group setting can be very helpful because you have distractions but in a controlled scenario, and the other dog owners understand what you're working on. If you are committed to attending a class every week, it will also help you stick to a consistent training schedule at home. The instructor of the class will also be able to give you some tips after observing you and your unique dog.

Tip #7: Pick up your speed!

Try adding some running with your dog, even if just for a few minutes on each walk. Or, walk at a faster pace. Dogs are much faster than us. They must think we move painfully slow! If you can speed up, this will help your dog maintain a loose leash.

Tip #8: Try different types of treats/food.

If you use the same, predictable treats all the time your dog might not be as interested in training. It's a good idea to mix things up every now and then. Try different types of treats/food like bits of hot dogs, jerky, ham, cheese, store bought treats, etc.

You can also try carrying a toy to reward your dog if that helps him focus better. Perhaps a squeaky toy or a rope toy. (For some dogs, a toy just makes them too excited and unable to focus!)

What to Do if Your Dog Barks or Lunges

How to stop your dog from barking at people, other dogs, cars or other distractions on walks

One of the most common training questions I get is "How can I stop my dog from growling at other dogs on walks?" Because this is so common, I decided it needed its own section in this book.

Your dog might be doing pretty well on loose-leash walking until … you come across other dogs … or strangers or bikers or whatever it might be. In many cases, dogs will pull, bark, growl, whine or even lunge when they see other dogs.

Don't worry, I'm here to help you through some of these issues. Of course, if you're really struggling with your dog, it's worth it to **hire a local trainer in your area to help.** It's not worth putting up with the stress all on your own, especially if you're worried your dog could bite someone or bite another dog. Walking your dog should be fun, not something you dread. So if you need help from someone who can actually observe you and your dog, please do so!

In the meantime, I'm going to give you some ideas that can help.

If your dog tends to bark at certain "triggers" the following concept should help you no matter what your dog is barking at whether it's strangers, other dogs, bikes, strollers or cars.

Step 1: Determine your dog's exact "triggers."

A common reason for dogs to bark on walks is due to **fear.** Your dog could be afraid of men or other dogs or children or people wearing backpacks or whatever it might be. They can be afraid of just about anything!

Besides fear, dogs could also bark at people due to:

Excitement. "Hey! A person! I love people! Yay!"

Frustration (due to excitement). For example, not being able to reach that person fast enough due to being on a leash. Or not being able to play with another dog due to being restrained by the leash. This is why some dogs appear aggressive only when on a leash. When they're off leash, they might be totally fine!

Guarding instincts. Some dogs feel responsible for "guarding" their people or the other dogs in your family. Sometimes, this "guarding" behavior also stems from fear. For example, your dog may be afraid of strange men so she feels the need to protect you from these "threats."

Sensitivity to noise or movement. Some dogs tend to bark or lunge at certain sounds or movements. For example, people on skateboards often make a loud sound as they're rolling down the street. And people on bikes are obviously moving much faster than normal. Some dogs will feel nervous around anything with "wheels" and will bark or pull. This might be even more common if you have a herding breed such as a shepherd or collie.

Try to pinpoint exactly when your dog reacts. For example, "Honey barks at men wearing hats or tall men once they are 10 feet away." Or, "Bentley barks at children once they are 15 feet away, especially if they are running or on bikes."

Your dog might have 5 or 6 different triggers! Brainstorm with family members or roommates so you get the most accurate list.

Action Step:

Make a specific list of your dog's exact triggers.

Step 2: Find a highly valued food reward your dog loves.

As I said earlier, dry dog biscuits might not cut it. You may need to use hot dogs, string cheese, pieces of real steak or hamburger. For actual dog treats, I find that Zuke's minis work well for most dogs. For others, a squeaky toy or a ball might work better.

Find something your dog is willing to work for even under stress. Ideally, you'll find something that can be broken easily into little pieces about the size of a piece of dry dog food. That way you can pop numerous treats into your dog's mouth very quickly.

Also, don't forget your treat pouch! You're going to need it!

Step 3: Use the right training collar and walk your dog at your side.

The best training collar or harness will be different for each dog depending on all sorts of factors like your own comfort level, the size of your dog and what makes it easiest for you to control your unique dog.

Some options for training collars include:

- a slip collar (choke collar)
- a martingale collar (limited slip collar)
- a no-pull harness

I'll go over more details on the different collars at the end of this guide.

The reason the right training collar is important is so you have control over your dog and can prevent pulling and lunging without harming your dog.

If your dog tends to bark at other dogs or people, I also recommend you keep your dog at your side the best you can. This is because if your dog is at your side he will be easier to control. You won't have to "reel him in" if you come across a trigger.

Your dog will also generally be calmer if he's at your side because he's less likely to be out in front ready to "protect" you or ready to greet other dogs.

Step #4: Master the emergency "U-turn"

There will unfortunately be those moments when you come across another dog, biker or whatever it might be when you are unprepared. For example, you might see another dog as you turn a corner or approach a blind intersection. Your dog might be doing well on training until - YIKES, another dog right there in her face!

For these moments, it's helpful to either calmly and quietly move to the side and away from the other dog OR to quickly do a "U-turn" by physically turning into your dog and moving her away as needed. It's almost always best to put your body between your dog and the other dog.

You can even gently bump into your dog as sort of a "body block." Gently bumping your dog back is typically more effective than trying to pull your dog away. When we pull on our dogs' collars, they tend to resist this tension and pull even harder!

Always try to stay calm, even as you are moving away from your dog's trigger. Once you've created some distance, you can hold a high-valued treat to your dog's nose and ask her to do something simple like "sit" or "watch me." Reward her for being calm.

Yes, you're going to have setbacks like this, and that's OK. It's a work in progress. You might be doing really well for weeks and then all the sudden an off-leash dog comes charging up to you and sets you back a few weeks. This is life. Just keep on working with your dog and you will seem some improvements.

Step 5: Work with your dog on basic commands within her threshold.

Head out for a walk with your dog using your dog's training collar, treats and your treat pouch.

Seek out her "triggers" (other dogs, bikers, strollers, etc.) but stop just far enough away so she doesn't bark or react. While your dog is still calm but the "trigger" is in sight, give her several small treats one after the other. Then, TURN AND LEAVE before you get close enough to trigger a reaction.

You want your dog to think, "Wait! Why are we leaving? I want more treats!"

Eventually, you want your dog to associate her "trigger" with treats instead of fear. Like, "Oh, kids on bikes! That's great! Where's my string cheese?"

The goal is to change her emotional response over time. Make sure you do not rush your training. *Very slowly* increase the challenge over several weeks.

I also realize finding these perfect scenarios is easier said than done. You can't always predict when another dog will be walking towards you (or when one will appear right around the corner). Depending on where you live and what seems to trigger a reaction from your dog, some people will have an easier time than others. You're going to have to get creative.

Some examples that might work:

- Walking your dog in an open area like a soccer field with a small amount of foot traffic. You can see pretty far and move closer or further away to people and dogs.

- Walking in your own neighborhood at quieter times in the day like weekday later mornings. You know the neighborhood well and where there are other dogs.

Bonus tip: Sign up for a group obedience class

As I said earlier, it's well worth it to sign up for a beginning obedience class, even if you already know how to train your dog. Generally, a group class setting can be helpful because you get to practice around distractions in a controlled setting. The other dog owners won't bother you because they will be focused on their own dogs.

On the other hand, a group setting is too much for some dogs. I recommend you go and observe a class without your dog and talk to the instructor to see if your dog is a good fit.

Regardless, you should work on general obedience training with your dog with or without a group class. Things like sit, down, stay, come and also trick training build *confidence, self-control and trust.*

If your dog has the self-control to follow "sit" or "stay", he will have an easier time remaining calm in "high stress" situations like passing another dog.

So, always continue to work on training. Like I said earlier, it's always a work in progress, but it pays off.

The Best Gear - Finding the Right Collar and Leash

Now that we've covered the training tips, I want to share more details on the different types of collars and leashes available. The "right" collar for one dog will not necessarily be the best collar for all dogs.

No matter which type of collar or harness you choose, the goal is to find the right tool that gives you more control without harming your dog. Here is some information to help you decide.

If you have questions, feel free to email me at Lindsay@MightyPaw.com and I'll help you find the best tool for your situation.

Training Collars and Harnesses

Martingale collars ("limited slip" collars)

A <u>martingale collar</u> is a good option for a wide variety of dogs because it can help limit your dog's pulling without choking your dog. It's designed to tighten *slightly* under tension but it's limited on how far it can tighten.

At the same time, a martingale collar allows you to tug gently on the leash to get your dog's attention when needed. This is not meant to hurt your dog but to help her re-focus. Then, you can praise her for paying attention.

Martingale styles:

<u>Chain/nylon martingale collar:</u> I tend to prefer this option because I like the look of it! The nylon is comfortable on the dog, yet the chain piece makes a soft "zzttt" sound when you need to get your

dog's attention. Mighty Paw's version of this collar is also adjustable so you can get the right fit.

All-nylon martingale collar: This is similar to the collar above but is made of all nylon. Mighty Paw's all-nylon collar is adjustable so you can easily get the right fit for your dog. It also has a buckle so you don't have to slide it over your dog's head when taking it on and off.

Leather martingale: Another version of the martingale but made with 100% genuine leather and a 100% stainless- steel chain. A stainless steel chain will not discolor your dog's fur and will not rust or tarnish over time.

Slip collar ("choke collar")

A slip collar is similar to a martingale collar. It will tighten under pressure or if you give a gentle tug to get your dog's attention. The goal with this type of collar is to allow it to release immediately after it tightens. The gentle tension should be used to get your dog's attention, not to hurt or choke your dog.

No-pull harness ("front-clip harness")

If you prefer to use a harness, you definitely want to choose one that has a leash attachment D-ring at the front of the harness at the dog's **chest**. When the leash is clipped to your dog's chest, the harness will limit your dog's ability to pull because it gently guides him to the side.

Our Mighty Paw sport harness has a clip at the front of the harness and on the top of the harness.

When the leash is clipped to the top of the harness on your dog's back, it's much easier for your dog to pull. That's not necessarily a bad thing, depending on what you're doing, but for the sake of this ebook we're trying to teach your dog NOT to pull. So go with a harness that has a front-clip option.

Leashes

For the most part, you can't go wrong with a standard 6-foot leash when you're training and walking your dog.

I recommend two options:

A double-handle leash: I recommend a 6-foot double handle leash because this type of leash has a loop handle at the end of the leash and a second handle closer to your dog's collar (often called a "traffic lead").

With this type of leash, you can hold the end in one hand and when you need a little extra control, you can grab the second handle closer to your dog's collar with your other hand. This is especially helpful when you have a big dog, a dog who tends to bark at other dogs or a strong "puller."

A leather leash: A leather leash is easier on your hands if you have a strong puller. Many trainers recommend leather leashes for this reason. It's' really a matter of personal preference if you go with nylon vs. leather.

Other Products

Treat pouch: Well, by now you know how I feel about a treat pouch! A treat pouch makes carrying treats so much easier. You don't have to stuff your pockets full of smelly, greasy dog treats, and the pouch is much easier to access. Plus, it can also hold your keys or phone (separately from the treats of course).

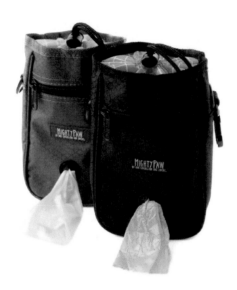

It's time to get started!

Now that I've given you some guidance on how to teach your dog not to pull, I'm excited for you to get started! Remember to be patient with your dog and with yourself. Teaching your dog not to pull on the leash takes a lot of time and consistency, but you will get there!

Still have questions?

As you begin training your dog, you might run into some unexpected problems or you might have a few questions. If you'd like some support from other dog lovers, I hope you'll join our Facebook group, the Mighty Paw Fur-lings.

The Fur-lings are a welcoming bunch, and in the group you can post your questions, meet other dog owners or offer suggestions to others. Sometimes dog training really is a team effort! We are here to support you and your pup.

Remember to have fun!

Let us know how you're doing!

-Lindsay

MightyPaw.com

You are part of the Mighty Paw family now! Take **30% off** your next order at MightyPaw.com! Just visit MightyPaw.com/EbookFamily to get your code now!

Made in the USA
San Bernardino, CA
16 November 2019

59990277R00033

Stop My Dog's Pulling

Confidently Walk Your Dog Anywhere

By Lindsay Stordahl
MightyPaw.com

Introduction

Hello dog lovers! Welcome to the <u>Mighty Paw</u> family! I'm glad you're here. The end goal with this ebook is for you to have a dog who walks nicely on the leash *without* pulling.

You might not care if your dog marches perfectly at your left side in a formal "heel" position, but I know you'd prefer walks without your dog straining your arms and back!

Not only do you want to *enjoy* walks with your best friend, but you also want the well-mannered dog everyone admires. You want to be able to *confidently* walk your dog almost anywhere - around different people, other dogs, through the park, through the city, the beach - anywhere!

You've probably heard the term "loose-leash walking" before, and I'll be using that a lot in this book. When I say "loose-leash walking" I